Isabella Skiba, Rahel Züger

Barrier-Free Planning

Isabella Skiba, Rahel Züger

Barrier-Free Planning

Third edition

BIRKHÄUSER
BASEL

Contents

IN CONCLUSION _71

APPENDIX _72

Foreword

Equal opportunities for the maximum number of people are a vital goal for any society. The status enjoyed by people of different social groups, different ages or different abilities in a society often depends on a collective vision, together with the personal situations of those concerned. Equal opportunity is not only a political or educational concept; it also applies to our physical surroundings. The way public areas are designed and the way public life is organised significantly determine who can play an active role.

Architects and urban and landscape planners must therefore consider the needs of people with limitations and help them to live independent and self-determined day-to-day lives. In this context, barrier-free planning means building so as to created no barriers or hurdles for disabled people, children or older people.

This book, *Basics Barrier-Free Planning*, was created as a basic living environment design reference guide. The authors provide clear descriptions of any relevant limitations that users might suffer from, and how parts of the built environment can become barriers to someone with these limitations. In view of the fact that it is becoming mandatory to incorporate the principles of barrier-freedom within architectural projects, this third edition not only contains updated contents, but also practical information on design for barrier-freedom. Taking this as the context, they identify planning-related needs for different user groups. The book turns the principles of limited mobility-aware design into a practical guide for the design process, making it an essential handbook for any prospective architect.

Bert Bielefeld, Editor

The aim of planning and building regulations is generally to equip buildings, adapt living environments and optimize workplaces for the needs of the "average person". Statistically, most people fit this planning model, which is why it forms the basis for the constructed environment in the first place, but it leaves a significant "non-average" sector of the population unable to take full advantage of their constructed environment, excluded from many areas of mainstream society and hindered in their day-to-day lives. Every person has the right to a living space that they can use independently, largely unaided and without restrictive barriers. This barrier-free living space should extend beyond their own homes to include their whole living environment and every social setting. Beyond the construction situation, freedom from barriers is a part of the concept of human equality. The central principle is that a person is not inherently disabled, but disability is generated through their surroundings. The most fundamental aspects of building, product, and services design are described by the terms Universal Design and Design for All and have been defined as basic human rights in the UN Convention on the Rights of Persons with Disabilities.

Groups of people with various limitations to their mobility, information or communication within their environment have particular needs. These groups include: People with limitations

— people with impaired <u>mobility</u> (e.g. people unable to walk easily, older people or unusually small or tall people)
— people with limited <u>perception</u>, such as blind and visually impaired people, or those who are Deaf or have partial or profound hearing impairment
— people with <u>cognitive</u> impairments such as mental illness, impaired speech, learning difficulties, or dementia

People whose impairment is not long-term—such as a temporary loss of mobility and the associated limitation of independence—may also need help to cope with their environment. These include children, who see the world differently from adults, pregnant women or parents with pushchairs trying to navigate a parked-up street, and people with temporarily impaired mobility due to illness or injury—a broken bone or a sprain, for instance.

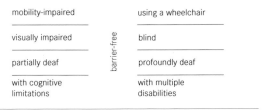

mobility-impaired		using a wheelchair
visually impaired	barrier-free	blind
partially deaf		profoundly deaf
with cognitive limitations		with multiple disabilities

Fig. 1: Multi-dimensional "barrier-free" model

Barrier-free goals

All these groups require support above and beyond the requirements of the average person to lead active day-to-day lives. The aim of barrier-free design measures is to integrate these groups into mainstream life.

The equality aspect has been recognized by many states and by international organizations as a basic right, often enshrined in law. This has also led to a greater awareness of special needs in the general population, helping to make barrier-free planning of buildings and street spaces part of the standard planning parameters.

Demographic development

A population's demographic development plays an important role. If a society is steadily growing older, homes will increasingly have to be adapted to the needs of older people. If, on the other hand, birth rates are rising, childcare places and public play areas will be a social priority. Shifts in the age pyramid are often caused by social, political or economic changes, and can be predicted several years in advance. > Fig. 3

The development of the population is also subject to short-term changes, which can be triggered by the migration of people motivated by political or economic concerns.

Lifespan

Needs change throughout a person's lifespan. Requirements for children's and elderly people's housing differ significantly from those for people in their middle years. Barrier-free planning therefore means thinking ahead and building for the future—not only meeting the present needs of users, but creating living spaces that can easily and safely be used by children or adapted for people who are old or have restricted mobility.

Barrier-free concept

Many countries have passed legislation that establishes barrier-free design as a mandatory requirement. This may require applicants to submit barrier-free concepts with their building applications, thus providing further details of the concept in text and drawings. > Fig. 4

In the written part, the requirements for the building and the approach to it are described and any deviations are explained. The idea is to state and implement the protection objectives of the respective groups of persons.

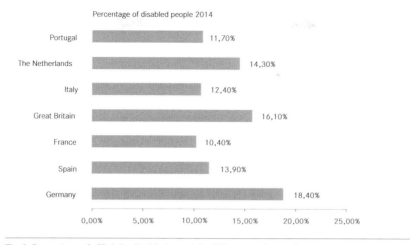

Fig. 2: Percentage of officially disabled people in different societies (Source: EUROSTAT 2016)

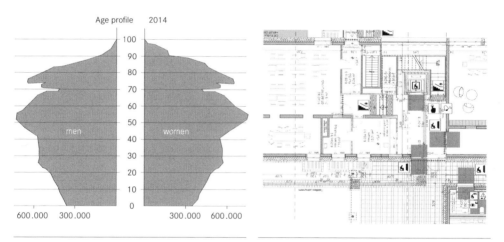

Fig. 3: Demographic pyramid, Germany 2019
(Source: Destatis, 2019)

Fig. 4: Example of a plan with a barrier-free concept

○ **Note:** With the UN Convention on the Rights of Persons with Disabilities, which was agreed in 2008, many states committed to granting disabled people the same rights and opportunities within their society as non-disabled people. Furthermore, many states have passed legislation that ensures equal rights to people with disabilities, such as the German Equal Opportunities for People with Disabilities Act.

○ **Note:** The drawings will show guiding lines and attention fields for guide systems for visually impaired persons, movement areas in front of doors and elevators, staircase markings, step markings etc. Automatic door systems, operating elements, and orientation aids are indicated with symbols.

Impairments and disabilities

An overview of different impairments may help the reader to understand the specific needs of disabled people or others with special requirements. These may be due to physical or mental conditions, and may be congenital and present at birth or appear in later life—due to illness, accident or ageing, for instance.

Different degrees of impairment
Impairments range from minor to serious disability, and a person may have multiple disabilities. Debilitating age gradually limits mobility, particularly if several illnesses coincide. There are fundamental difficulties in estimating the limitations and needs of a disabled person, as this depends on the individual indicators and abilities of the person involved.

However, in order to provide the understanding of the needs of disabled people that a designer must have, individuals' abilities and limitations will be categorized as follows:

— Motor impairments / movement and mobility
— Sensory impairments / sensory perception
— Cognitive impairments / mental processing and memory

MOTOR IMPAIRMENTS

Motor impairments affect a person's mobility and means of locomotion. Visible causes include malformation of or damage to limbs, but damage to the central nervous system, muscles or skeleton can also cause motor dysfunction.

Cerebral damage
Brain damage (cerebral damage) can also disrupt locomotion without necessarily causing mental impairment. Most cases that are not caused either before or during birth are the result of a stroke, often causing one side of the body to be paralyzed. Depending on its type and severity, damage from illness and accident may cause varying degrees of spastic paralysis, with disrupted coordination, spastic paralysis of one or more limbs, or paralysis on one or both sides of the body.

○ **Note:** Estimated values given in this book (e.g. the movement area needed by a wheelchair user) should therefore be taken as practical recommendations rather than precise measurements. Different countries will also have different regulations.

■ **Tip:** Anyone planning with disabled people in mind must be aware of their day-to-day experience. Many kinds of disability can be recreated using devices that restrict vision or clothing that restricts movement or by using a wheelchair to gain personal experience of the impairments involved.

Spinal damage often causes paralysis of the lower and/or upper extremities. Paraplegia, caused by damage to nerve fibers along the spine, may create motor or sensory restrictions or impair vegetative function. The effects appear to varying degrees, alone or as multiple disabilities.

Spinal damage

The vegetative nervous system controls the vital functions, meaning that damage to the spine can reduce reflex activity and individual organ systems' efficiency, impairing bladder and digestive tract function, heart and blood circulatory function, and body temperature regulation. Insufficient heart and circulatory function, for instance, causes shortness of breath and a tendency to tire quickly, thus restricting the patient's activity radius.

Vegetative nerve system damage

Small or large size may be caused by hereditary factors, fetal damage or pathological growth disorders. Factors that apply to small people also apply to children. In this case, the major limitation is the inability to reach high objects.

Small or large size

SENSORY IMPAIRMENTS

Sensory impairments involve sight, hearing, touch, smell and taste, some of which are relevant to barrier-free living and working space design.

Visual impairment describes varying degrees of restricted vision, ranging from mild visual impairment to complete blindness. It includes color blindness and night blindness. > Figs. 5 and 6

Visual impairment

Hearing impairment ranges from mild to profound deafness, with impaired hearing at birth also disrupting speech centre development and possibly the sense of balance and direction, causing imbalance and dizziness. Deaf people may also have difficulty knowing where signals are coming from, meaning that simultaneous noises (e.g. people talking and traffic noise) overtax their perception. Furthermore, they often do not perceive warning signals or indications of danger, such as the noise from an approaching car, in the same way as people with normal hearing.

Hearing impairment

Haptic perception refers to touch in the broad sense and the processing of touch-related stimuli in the brain. Haptic perceptions, and related impairments, can be divided into two groups. Exteroception describes tactile perception—touch, pressure or vibration, as well as temperature and pain sensations. Proprioception describes the introverted perception of one's own body—particularly the senses of position, force and movement. This makes proprioception important for coordinated and controlled movements such as walking.

Haptic impairment

Fig. 5: Orientation in a public access area with normal vision

Fig. 6: Restricted vision picture (cataract + macular degeneration)

Other senses

In rare instances, olfactory disorders (of the sense of smell) or gustatory disorders (of the sense of taste) have to be taken into account when designing buildings. For instance, a person with limited sense of smell may become aware of fire or gas escapes too late by failing to notice the smell of fire or gas.

COGNITIVE IMPAIRMENTS

Cognitive disorders affect information processing. Information from all the senses mentioned above must be filtered, processed and evaluated by the brain. Cognitive faculties include thought processes in the broad sense—e.g. learning and remembering, recognition and visualization, and formulating conclusions and judgments as well as plans and wishes.

Cognitive disorders can cause several impairments—memory dysfunction, thought dysfunction, autism, impaired social abilities, or abnormal behavior. These are often coupled with other motor or sensory disorders. One dysfunction, dementia, is associated with growing older. Alzheimer's disease is the most common manifestation. In dementia patients, cognitive processes within the brain are slowed. About 30% of those over 90 suffer from some form of dementia, with 2/3 more women than men affected. All sufferers have cognitive impairments, which can lead to changes in emotional control, social behavior and motivation. Given present demographic developments, the next few decades will see an increase in the overall dementia rate.

Any independent living-centered planning project must be appropriate to individuals' abilities and limitations.

Types of barrier

For people both with long-term impairments and with temporary special needs (e.g. children, pregnant women, or ill people), everyday life is filled with partial or total barriers to independence, often in the built environment. This chapter includes a guide to understanding and recognizing some typical kinds.

BARRIERS TO MOBILITY

In constructed surroundings, people with limitations often encounter mobility barriers, such as changes in ground level, inadequate area for movement, or overly narrow corridors. Matters that are quite trivial to the average citizen can present a serious impediment to disabled people, who may also have limited physical strength, speed of movement, balance or coordination.

Overcoming differences in levels is a major difficulty in the daily lives of people with motor limitations. Vertical barriers are present in all areas of life. Using public transport, for instance, may be impossible without special unobstructed access. A high curb or step may be a barrier for people who have difficulties in walking and for parents with pushchairs, as well as for wheelchair users.

Height differences

■

Barriers are also ubiquitous in personal living and working environments. Front drives and entrances to houses, the thresholds of doors or balconies and upstairs areas are the obvious examples. Often, however, small details that would go unnoticed by anyone not sensitized to disabled people's needs represent barriers. For instance, uneven paving on an access path may obstruct wheelchairs, and getting into a bathtub or shower cubicle may be an insurmountable obstacle.

■ **Tip:** To develop an awareness of barriers in everyday life, it helps to imagine how a blind person or wheelchair user, for instance, would cope with the same daily schedule. With this in mind, one could trace the path taken by a disabled person using a subway, visiting a shop or using public services.

Fig. 7: Stairs, an impassable barrier for a wheelchair user

Fig. 8: A gutter, representing a barrier and danger in a public area

Passage and movement areas People using aids such as walking frames or wheelchairs need wider transit and movement areas than non-disabled people, as they may not be able to edge past a parked car blocking the pavement or move to the other side of the street. > Fig. 9 Public buildings and public transport access routes must be wide enough and horizontally level.

To be independent, people with motor restrictions need adequate space for movement in their own living and working environment. This applies to the width and extension of transport and activity areas—hallways, doorways and window areas, working spaces and the areas around furnishings and sanitary objects. The aisles in halls and other common spaces are generally wide enough, but the passages between rooms present a bottleneck for people with walking frames or wheelchairs, and are made more arduous by the need to open doors. Getting through revolving doors and doors that open into the space occupied by a wheelchair is very difficult—the only way is to operate the door handle from a sitting position while pushing the wheelchair back at the same time. > Fig. 10

Fig. 9: Barrier created by a parked-up pavement and a building site

Fig. 10: Revolving door, representing a barrier for wheelchair users

BARRIERS TO OPERATING CONTROLS

In addition to adequate transit and movement areas, barrier-free building plans require anthropometric user control and visual information placement.

Their different perspective on their surroundings means that wheelchair users, children or unusually small or tall people have difficulties with controls meant for people of average size. This applies to door and window catches, doorbells, light switches, electrical sockets, thermostats, sanitary objects with controls (taps, flush controls, showers), kitchens, and lift controls. Any controls horizontally out of arm's reach or too high up are unsuitable for people with disabilities. Any special

○

Control placement

○ **Note:** Anthropometry means measuring and working to the form and dimensions of the human body—body size and weight, and torso, arm and leg length. Anthropometric adjustment means, for instance, designing workspaces or furniture to match a person's proportions. Anthropometric considerations are particularly important when planning for people who have motor impairments or who are unusually large or small.

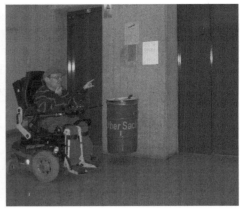

Fig. 11: Controls out of the reach of children

Fig. 12: Lift call button, too high up and obstructed by furniture

arrangements, however, do have a disadvantage: controls mounted at an unusual height rather than in the expected places may in turn create a barrier for blind and visually impaired people. > Figs. 11 and 12

Ergonomic barriers   The design of any fixture, control or piece of furniture has an impact on people with limitations. A small keypad for a lift or an access control system, for instance, may be inoperable by people with a motor or haptic impairment, or hard to find by people with a visual impairment. Without aids such as handrails or seating, long routes may be arduous for old or ill people. Sanitary facilities without grab handles or seating may also be impossible to use unaided. Work surfaces or washbasins with cabinets fitted underneath make elements such as the taps harder for people in wheelchairs to reach.

BARRIERS TO ORIENTATION

Deprived of certain sensory information, people with sensory impairments in particular have problems orienting themselves. The barriers involved vary depending on which sense is entirely or partially absent, and may be insurmountable without outside help.

Visual barriers   Most everyday information is visual—sight is our most important means of perception. Consequently, even mild visual impairment can cause problems if public transport information such as the names of stops, information signs or the name on a bell is presented in very small type.

More severe visual impairment makes orientation in the street or in buildings more difficult, as a person may be able to perceive only colors or contrasts. Environments with little contrast or a multitude of colors may then be impossible to assess spatially and make difficult to assimilate information. Blind people have far more barriers to overcome. With no visual aids to finding the way, they have to depend solely on hearing, smell and haptic perception. Orientation is particularly difficult in undifferentiated or unfamiliar streets and interior spaces. Any change in a space is a threat, disrupting a blind person's calculations in finding their way by memory.

■

Partially or profoundly deaf people encounter auditory barriers in any kind of communication. In a public space, potentially dangerous events that hearing people would be aware of even if they happened out of sight will not be apparent to people with hearing impairment. Auditory information such as public transport announcements, doorbells or warning signals (fire alarms, sirens) is not effective for them even though it can potentially save the lives of those with normal hearing. | Auditory barriers

This kind of barrier should be removed by providing information to two different senses. This two-sense principle, or alternative perception, makes orientation and learning easier by allowing hearing, sight and touch to compensate for each other: | The two-sense principle

— Instead of sight = hearing and touch/feel
— Instead of hearing = sight and touch/vibration

This principle applies particularly to alarms, emergency services calls, and alarm announcement systems. It is also useful for general information-giving and communication.

■ **Tip:** To understand the problems of blind people in a visual world, it helps to try walking familiar and unfamiliar routes blindfold, accompanied by a guide. This personal experiment will reveal the large number of barriers, obvious and less so, encountered by blind people in their environment.

Planning requirements

Above all, barrier-free planning should improve the lives of people with limitations or impairments by addressing their needs. In this sense, a barrier-free building design enables disabled people to use the building independently and easily. The first question contained within a planning assignment is who the future users will be:

— Planning for an individual: adaptation for the needs of a specific person
— Planning for a group: a plan tailored to a certain average user profile
— Planning for non-specific users: taking into account, as far as possible, the needs of people with different requirements

Planning for an individual

If the planning assignment is to plan a home, for instance, for a particular person, then it can be precisely adapted to the user profile. In this case, an individual with limitations can be included in the planning process and can explain his/her needs, and the planner can build up a picture by accompanying the user through his/her daily routine. This means that planning can be tailored exactly to the specific abilities and limitations of the person in question. Any needs in future life as well as present needs must be planned for. People become older and lose mobility, so that even an individually created plan must contain some flexibility for the future.

Planning for a group

If a specific target group is being planned for, the planner must focus on the average requirements of this group. In particular, buildings such as kindergartens, care homes for elderly people and special needs schools—schools for visually impaired children, for instance—must match the needs of users with and without limitations (including visitors and staff). Multiple disabilities, creating highly individual and specialized needs, can also be problematic, as they mean that that buildings will not be barrier-free for certain people despite being adapted to the major disability.

Planning for non-specific users

If a location is used by many different people, it must be made barrier-free for as many people as possible. This applies to all public outdoor space and transport space and public buildings such as government buildings, healthcare facilities, leisure facilities etc. It includes anyone whose limitations allow some degree of independent mobility. Inevitably, however, individuals with specific abilities will sometimes encounter barriers. Removing barriers for some users may also create barriers for others.

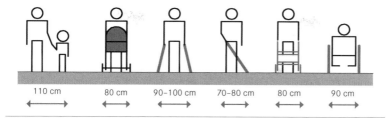

| 110 cm | 80 cm | 90–100 cm | 70–80 cm | 80 cm | 90 cm |

Fig. 13: Space needed by different people with special mobility needs

Some typical user profiles for people with limitations are reproduced here. Children and unimpaired older people are included, since planning for these groups involves similar issues. The parameters given in this book should be adapted to the specific situation, especially when planning for a single individual.

PLANNING FOR CHILDREN

Children perceive space in an entirely different way from adults, from a different physical and mental perspective. For them, the adult world, which they conquer step by step, is full of barriers and impediments. The height of controls such as door handles or switches, sanitary objects and furniture creates particular difficulties at first. It is rare for homes to be tailored to the needs of children, as their development and growth would necessitate constant adjustment, and daily challenges are important for the development of children's motor skills. User profile

Most plans tailored to the needs of children involve care homes for children (kindergartens, daycare, leisure facilities) or public play areas. Elementary schools also address the different growth phases of pupils to some degree by using child-sized sanitary systems, controls and furniture, as well as windows and parapets at a child's height. > Figs. 14 and 15 Planning assignments

Installing objects they will need to use at an appropriate height fosters children's self-confidence from an early age. However, the different stages of growth mean that one should keep in mind the age at which children become able to learn how to use controls easily and safely, before using normal-height door handles or toilets. Some buildings may need low washbasins and toilets or a second handrail or door handle for children. Barriers to falling that cannot be climbed over should also be provided. Even staircases leading down can be dangerous to small children. Sharp edges or objects over which children might stumble should also be avoided. Planning principles

Fig. 14: Washbasins for children at different heights   Fig. 15: Window sills at the right height for toddlers and small children

Children's temporary height-related requirements are long-term considerations in the living spaces of unusually small people. Unusually small or tall people need door, window and cupboard handles, and controls such as lift controls and light switches, at special heights, and with different clearance spaces for rooms and doors. Sometimes they will need more space at a lower level to make up for the high cupboards they cannot use as storage space.

PLANNING FOR OLDER PEOPLE

User profile   A person's living, working and leisure space needs change as they progress from childhood to old age. The living space of older people with none of the impairments described above may still have to be adapted for any future restricted mobility. This means, for instance, that rooms should be functionally and constructively able to accommodate any equipment to help with motor and sensory limitations, and any essential
○ services and care facilities should be available nearby.

○ **Note:** People transferring to accommodation for the elderly are often reluctant to give up too much of their home comforts. If at all practicable, ageing with dignity in one's own home, with its memories of a long life, is vastly preferable to a furnished room in a care home with a fixed schedule.

Flexible living plans and various leisure, sport and rehabilitation Planning assignments facilities are typical planning assignments for older people.

Residential facilities may be care schemes where people can remain in their own homes with easy access to essential services, or residential complexes comprehensively designed for older people. Planning assignments include adapting existing individual homes and building homes and residential communities for older people or classical care homes. Generational housing, in which people of different ages share the same accommodation, also plays an increasing role in public discussion.

Cultural, sport and leisure opportunities and converted urban space for older people are increasingly important, particularly in ageing societies. This means addressing the interests and needs of this population group as well as issues such as wheelchair accommodation.

Planning a living space for older people basically means creating a Planning principles comfortable, familiar living environment where technological systems such as lifts to help the user to cope with any future limitations, while being inconspicuous, are readily available or can at least be retrofitted. Possible construction modifications include leveled floor plans, widened doors, fewer steps, enough movement space, baths suitable for disabled people, and power points for technological aids (e.g. emergency call buttons, lifts).

In mixed accommodation in particular, residents should be able to communicate with each other while retaining privacy and places where they can be alone.

○

Access and easy use of services beyond the personal living space (e.g. medical and care services, groceries etc.) and leisure facilities (e.g. cultural facilities, transport for older people, shopping and green spaces) are vital. Access to and usability of local public transport also affect the attractiveness of a residential neighborhood to older people.

○ **Note:** More information on residential facilities can be found in *Basics Design and Living* by Jan Krebs, Birkhäuser 2007. Information specific to older people can be found in *Living for the Elderly—A Design Manual* by Eckhard Feddersen and Insa Lüdtke, Birkhäuser 2009.

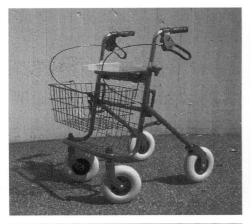

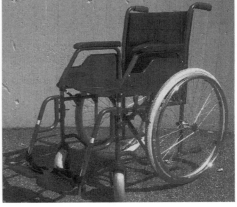

Fig. 16: Example of wheeled walker (rollator)   Fig. 17: Example of a wheelchair

PLANNING FOR MOBILITY-IMPAIRED PEOPLE AND WHEELCHAIR USERS

User profile   Regardless of their age, mobility-impaired people and wheelchair users place special requirements on their living environment and on public space. As they generally use aids to move around, routes within and outside of buildings must be adjusted to allow enough space for such

○ aids and adequate movement area. > Chapter Outdoor facilities, Pavements and open spaces, and Chapter Construction and technical requirements, Access elements

Aids   Depending on how limited a person's mobility is, walking support aids may include walking sticks, underarm crutches or walking frames. > Figs. 16 and 17 The different sizes of various models have to be kept in mind, as well as the extra space needed by a possible helper. > Fig. 18

When calculating movement areas, it should be borne in mind that many mobility aids do not allow for lateral movement. Statics calculations for electric wheelchairs must take into account
    their considerable weight – approx. 180 kg.

○ **Note:** Compared with other limitations, it is relatively easy to ensure that mobility needs are met within "normal" building and outdoor space planning. For this reason, barrier elimination is often—mistakenly—equated with wheelchair access in architecture.

24

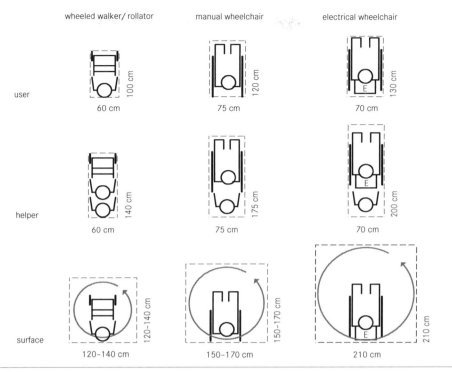

Fig. 18: Movement areas for people using mobility aids

People with limited mobility and wheelchair users have to be consid- Planning assignments ered in almost all public planning assignments: care homes for older people, public buildings, (government buildings, schools, cultural facilities etc.), medical facilities, leisure facilities, religious buildings and urban outdoor spaces. > Chapter Outdoor facilities

The major planning issues are the opportunities for movement and Planning principles the necessary movement space. Vertical barriers such as changes in ground level, steep slopes or steps should be avoided as far as possible, and any problem spots such as connecting corridors and the areas around doors should be designed to be large enough. The heights of work surfaces and controls such as switches and fittings, cupboard and window catches should also be adapted to the movement and reach radius of a wheelchair user. > Fig. 19

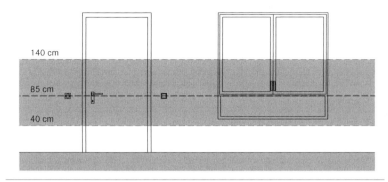

Fig. 19: Height of controls

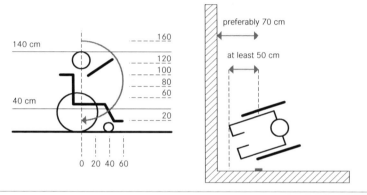

Fig. 20: Radius of reach for a wheelchair user

Elements that can be grasped for support make it easier for people with limited mobility to move securely and independently. When designing sanitary rooms in particular, certain provisions should be made, including wheelchair-accessible shower cubicles and washstands that a wheelchair can fit under. > Chapter Room plans, Baths and sanitary rooms Sufficient storage space for wheelchairs—and, in the case of electric wheelchairs, a charging station—should also be provided.

It is also important to take into account the field of vision and reach radius of a seated person. > Fig. 20 Fixtures, controls and windows should be arranged to be reached without stretching the spinal column too much.
> Chapter Construction and technical requirements, Construction components

Fig. 21: Using the Hoover cane as an aid to locomotion

Fig. 22: Danger spot for blind people caused by overhanging building component

PLANNING FOR VISUALLY IMPAIRED AND BLIND PEOPLE

As vision is most people's dominant sense, our environment is keyed to visual orientation and communication. Planning for visually impaired and blind people therefore means rethinking familiar everyday rituals. Visually impaired people encounter barriers that would never occur to someone with normal sight. Unlike wheelchair users, however, they face few spatial barriers to mobility as long as they can orient themselves and find their way without risk. Visually impaired and blind people have to construe the overall context from details, whereas sighted people are aware of the overall context first and the details second. For this reason, those directly concerned must be included in the planning process for any plan to succeed.

User profile

Traditional aids include the Hoover cane (or long white cane), specially trained guide dogs for blind people, and armbands to make others (such as motorists) aware of the person's condition. A Hoover cane is continually moved from side to side to detect any obstructions to forward movement. > Fig. 21 It also helps blind people to detect changes in footing. GPS devices can also be used to make moving around in public places easier. Owing to the widespread use of digital devices blind people now have a much wider range of aids at their disposal compared to 10 or 20 years ago.

Aids

Apart from specialized buildings such as schools for visually impaired people, this kind of planning usually involves an individual's living space and inclusion in public life, with orientation in outdoor public spaces, on public transport and in public buildings an especially important part of

Planning assignments

Fig. 23: Inadequately secured building sites – a danger to visually impaired or blind people

Fig. 24: Street elements present a danger of collision or tripping

barrier-free living for blind and visually impaired people. In the workplace, all tools with a visual aspect (computers, documents etc.) must be adapted. These days, most computer systems and many public websites offer barrier-free alternatives.

Planning principles
Visual limitations require hazards (e.g. props, projecting parts of buildings, changes in ground level) to be avoided or made as conspicuous as possible. Using color to mark danger spots helps people with limited vision, serving as a visual danger recognition prompt in the absence of possibly unreadable written signs (for marking garage forecourts or the different stories of a public building, for instance). At the same time, deep shadows should be avoided—rooms should be brightly lit with no glare.

Blind people's use of the Hoover cane to find their way means that any dangers at head or upper-body height must be marked by edging or similar at floor height. Tactile elements set into the paving as guidance lines can also open up larger areas to blind people.

Talking in-house systems (lifts) or simple auditory signals can replace optical perception, helping blind people to orient themselves within buildings. Tactile elements such as guidance lines on the walls and floor (in a contrasting material, for instance), plans marked out in relief, recognizable odor marking (e.g. carefully placed strong-smelling plants) or special script and symbols can help to improve orientation.

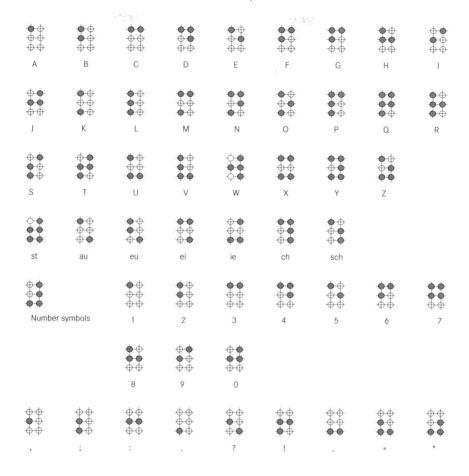

Fig. 25: Letters and numbers in Braille

Normal script (e.g. the story numbers in a lift) can be replaced by large characters or elevated relief, making the text readable to sighted, visually impaired and blind people. More detailed information should be given in Braille. This standardized dot script can be applied by stamping, cutting or insetting. > Fig. 25

Braille script

PLANNING FOR HEARING-IMPAIRED AND DEAF PEOPLE

User profile For partially or profoundly deaf people, the main barriers are to auditory communication, e.g. spoken information or auditory warning signals occurring in many everyday situations, at home and in public areas.

Aids Electronic hearing aids are used to compensate for hearing impairment. Because hearing is closely linked to balance, a wheelchair may also be needed. Hearing aids work by amplifying the incoming signal, with the disadvantage that they blend different sources of noise, which a person with normal hearing could easily distinguish, into auditory chaos.

Planning assignments As most human perception is predominantly visual, people with impaired hearing find moving around in a constructed environment easier than visually impaired people do. It follows that, aside from specialized buildings such as schools for deaf children, planning for hearing-impaired and profoundly deaf people is mainly concerned with details and constructive and technical components such as lifts and solely auditory alarm systems, which must be supplemented by visual signals such as warning lights.

Planning principles In public spaces, it is easy to provide visual equivalents to auditory signals (e.g. information signs). Auditory signals from road traffic, such as horns, are more of a problem. Hearing people are aware of vehicles outside their area of vision and can tell how fast they are going and if they are braking by the sound. Deaf people do not have this ability, making road traffic more dangerous to them. Living environment issues mainly involve in-house systems (doorbells, telephones and other domestic appliances), for which all auditory signals must be replaced with visual ones. In the world of work, auditory danger signals will be missed, meaning that fire alarms, for instance, should never be sound-only.

The diverse sounds in rooms such as restaurants and lecture theaters should be equalized using soundproofing (e.g. low reverberation and sound dampening systems) to minimize auditory chaos. Bright rooms with no shadows can also make lip-reading easier.

○ **Note:** In museums, theaters, cinemas or other public buildings, a loop system can send auditory signals directly to hearing aids, preventing any disruptive sounds or loss of quality.

PLANNING FOR PEOPLE WITH COGNITIVE IMPAIRMENTS

Many cognitively impaired people need personal care, as independent living is impossible. Such people depend on a spatial or social environment that allows or compensates for their difficulties and their individual behavior. Architecture and room plans are very important to their quality of life. People with learning difficulties or impaired speech, on the other hand, find it comparatively easy to overcome barriers. The spectrum of cognitive impairments makes it hard to define any general planning principles. General planning guidelines can however be provided for certain groups, such as dementia patients.

User profile

Planning for people with cognitive impairments is different from other kinds of barrier-free planning, as those affected—depending on their degree of impairment—cannot participate in society on their own, and need clearly structured living conditions. Unlike the planning assignments dealt with above, planning for people with cognitive impairments may mean deliberately excluding them from dangerous areas or the outside world in order to protect them or provide a sense of security.

Planning assignments

Apart from specialized schools, typical planning assignments involve every residential situation, ranging from integration in normal housing to homes for people with particular cognitive limitations (e.g. homes for people with dementia).

To aid memory, dementia patients' surroundings should be made up of simple, easily recognizable elements, with visually simple and easily navigable rooms, rather than large atria and intricate constructions. Hallways should be straight and not too long, and grouping rooms with similar functions together (e.g. cafe, dining room and common room) helps people to find their way. It is a good idea to have circular routes through inner hallways and secure outer areas to allow for the habitual wandering of dementia patients.

○

○ **Note:** The positive influence of a specially designed environment on patients is known as milieu therapy. Personally owned furniture, or at least some elements dating from before the patient fell ill, can help to reduce insecurity.

If patients need a carer in their home environment, extra personal spaces should be provided within the home to give the carer privacy, helping them to cope with the mental stresses involved.

Problems with dysfunctional temperature and pain perception caused by cognitive or sensory impairment often create an inability to regulate body temperature, which has to be compensated. It is important to exclude burn risks—by covering radiators and using automatic regulators for water heaters and room temperature, for instance.

Sharp edges and hard surfaces and other hazards should also be excluded as far as possible, as they are dangerous to anyone with disrupted proprioception > Chapter Impairments and disabilities, Sensory impairments or, for instance, epilepsy.

Construction and technical requirements

CONSTRUCTION COMPONENTS

Ceiling, wall and floor construction should match the needs of disabled people. This goes beyond the need for a step-free floorspace. Walls and ceilings must be constructed so that apparatus such as gripping, support and lifting devices can be attached without difficulty. This may consist of simple handrails, but could, for instance, include lift systems for bed transfer if a person can no longer independently move from wheelchair to bed.

Surfaces

Surface materials for the different components should be chosen based on the following properties:

— Mechanical properties such as strength, elasticity and hard-wearing properties
— Non-slip and anti-static properties
— Ease of care and cleaning
— Resistance to damp
— Sound-related properties such as degree of absorption
— Color scheme and degree of light-reflection

Wheelchair users and mobility-impaired, blind or elderly people need special floor covering. It should be warm to the feet in the living area, non-reflective, and have no electrostatic charge. It should also dampen the sound of footfalls and withstand any stresses from wheelchairs or walking sticks.

Floor coverings

All areas where a person has to move around, especially wet areas that are traversed with bare feet, must be non-slip. To avoid accidents, no thresholds or steps should be included in wet rooms, and any wet patches should be removed straight away. Any covers or floor drains should be level with the surrounding floor. Non-slip floor coverings must also be cleaned appropriately. The floor covering must guarantee sure footing. Non-slip materials are classified differently, according to their use. > Fig. 26 and Tab. 1

Non-slip protection

The firmness of floor coverings is important to anyone using a wheelchair. Reducing floor covering deformation prevents friction impeding travel. Coverings made from PVC, linoleum, ceramic tiles, parquet and other hard materials provide enough firmness for a wheelchair. Carpets, on the other hand, are only suitable under certain circumstances, and only if they are stuck down across their entire area.

Fig. 26: Nonslip floor tiles with profiling

Fig. 27: Contrasting floor design as one approaches a danger spot

Wall surfaces

Above all, walls must be sufficiently strong to withstand damage – from wheelchairs, for instance – and have enough loadbearing capacity to allow gripping and lifting apparatus to be installed. This is not a problem in the case of masonry or concrete walls, but lightly constructed walls need to be reinforced.

Surface design

■ ○

Wall surfaces should be easy to clean, with well-chosen colors and coverings. Different colors and materials can be used to make orientation easier. Colors are particularly important for visually impaired people. > Chapter Planning requirements, Planning for visually impaired and blind people

Acoustics and sound protection

Prolonged exposure to sound pressures can have a serious impact on disabled people. Acoustics and sound protection are particularly important to people with sensory impairment, because they need any remaining hearing for orientation and communication. > Chapter Planning requirements, Planning for hearing-impaired and deaf people Many deaf people are

■ **Tip:** Earthy colors are suitable as they are associated with good footing (e.g. a forest floor or wooden plank floor.) Shades of blue should be avoided – to older people suffering from dementia in particular, a blue floor looks wet and slippery.

○ **Note:** Color contrast means, for instance, a white strip on a dark background or black writing on a yellow background. Green on red or yellow on blue are unsuitable, as these look like indistinguishable shades of grey to color-blind people.

Table 1: Typical slip resistance classes

Use	Non-slip class
Outdoor areas	R10–R12
Outdoor parking areas	R10–R11
Outdoor ramps	R12
Inner entrance areas, stairs and hallways	R9–R10
Group rooms	R9–R10
Communal kitchens	R11–R12
Large kitchens	R12–R13
Sanitary rooms	R9–R11
Dry barefoot areas (e.g. changing rooms)	A
Shower areas, passages around swimming pools	B
Steps and ramps leading to water	C

unaware of how sound is affecting others, meaning that their televisions or radios may be turned up high and disturb neighbors. Buildings must therefore be planned for soundproofing, taking into account surface acoustics.

Doors

Doorways are narrow places and present a problem for disabled people. To allow wheelchair users to pass through safely, clearance should not be less than 90 cm and, for mechanically operated doors, not more than 100 cm. They should be at least 210 cm high, so that taller visually impaired people can be confident of having enough headroom.

It is important for blind people to be able to make out the doorframe by touch. Tactile markings in the floor covering can also help to indicate a door. For the benefit of visually impaired people, the color contrast between the door and the wall should be as great as possible. Transparent glass doors must be marked using stickers. Doors and door jambs should also be reinforced with a resistant material in areas at risk of wheelchair collision. Material

If the doors of houses or apartments need a threshold to provide insulation, it should be easy to drive a wheelchair over it, and should not be more than 2 cm high. Mechanical door insulation can be installed in the door itself and emerge when the door is closed.

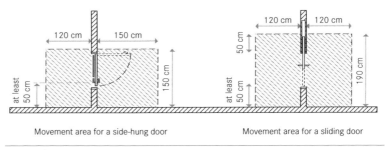

Movement area for a side-hung door   Movement area for a sliding door

Fig. 28: Movement areas near doors

Movement areas – movement sequences
Enough movement area must be provided on both sides of the door to allow disabled people to open doors themselves. > Fig. 28 For sliding doors, the space on each side must be greater, as the door catch changes position. It must always be possible to reach it.

depth of the door reveal
The depth of the door reveal should be kept to a minimum, preferably less than 26 cm, to ensure that wheelchair users can reach the door handle from their wheel chair. Where this is not possible, the space in front of the door should be at least 1.50 m wide. Alternatively, especially in existing buildings, it is also possible to install automatic door openers.

Power-operated doors
Power-operated doors are particularly easy to use for people with limited hand and arm function, wheelchair users and children because they are opened by an electrical impulse. The door's control must be outside its opening radius. The door should open in the direction of travel and allow enough time to pass through before it closes again. > Figs. 29–31

Safety provisions
Precautions regarding door closing are essential. Particularly in buildings meant for older people and young children, crush prevention should be in place. As well as protecting anyone in the doorway space, this involves safeguarding the hinged edge of the door. A light barrier or a cloth protector covering the space between door and doorjamb can be used to prevent fingers being trapped.

Controls
The process of passing through a door requires different handles on the hinge and inner sides of non-automatic doors. Controls at a height of 85 cm are easy for wheelchair users to reach. Pushbutton handles should have curved or U-shaped grips. A vertical grip bar that is accessible to wheelchair users as well as walking people should be attached on the

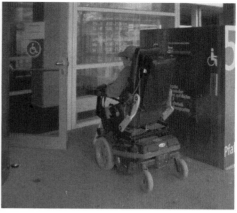

Fig. 29: Power-operated door with control on stand in front

Fig. 30: Power-operated door with integrated wall switch for wheelchair users

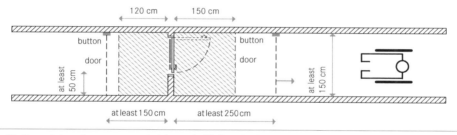

Fig. 31: Ground plan of a power-operated door suitable for wheelchair users

hinge side of the door so that it closes better. A horizontal grip bar at a height of 85 cm should be mounted on the inner side in addition to the actual door handle so that wheelchair users can pull the door shut behind them. > Fig. 32

To allow quick access in an emergency, it should be possible to open doors to sanitary rooms from the outside without pushing the door into the inner space. In the front doors of homes, adding a peephole (or "spyhole") at the right height for a wheelchair user helps occupants to feel secure.

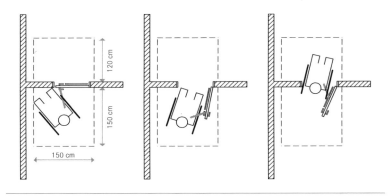

Fig. 32: Series of movements required to open and close the door

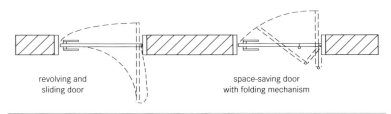

revolving and
sliding door

space-saving door
with folding mechanism

Fig. 33: Revolving sliding door and space-saving swing door

Special types of door

Special kinds of barrier-free doors include the particularly compact revolving sliding door or the space-saving swing door. > Fig. 33 Carousel or revolving doors are not suitable for disabled or older people. Where these are in place an extra door suitable for disabled people should be provided.

Entrance doors

A porch roof or recessed entrance keeps a building's entrance free of rain or drafts. Vestibules must have enough space between the inner and outer doors, usually a depth of at least 250 cm and width of 200 cm.

Shoescrapers should not lie loose on the floor. Instead, they should be inset on a level with the floor covering, to prevent stumbling and allow wheelchair users to clean their wheels. In this case, the scraper should be long enough for wheels to make a full revolution.

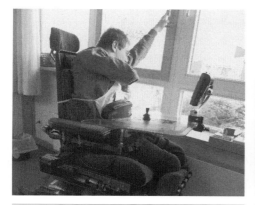

Fig. 34: Reaching the window catch is hampered by the radiator

Fig. 35: Full length window, secured and with handrail

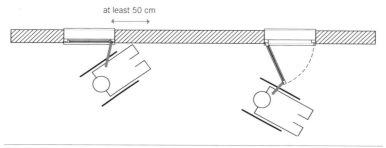

at least 50 cm

Fig. 36: Movement area needed to open a horizontally opening window

Windows

For mobility-impaired and older people, windows are a vital connection with the wider world. A well-positioned window significantly improves a room's atmosphere and quality as a living space.

Rather than being mounted centrally, the handle should be set as low as possible and within reach for a wheelchair user to open the window unaided. So that a light push is enough to close the window, it should not be too large, and the fittings should move without sticking. A radia- ○ tor beneath a window can make it harder to use. > Fig. 34

○ **Note:** For visually impaired or blind people, it is important that controls such as window handles in public buildings are always located in the same place, making them easier to find.

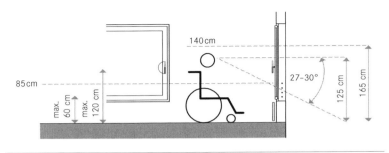

Fig. 37: Ideal arrangement of windows for a wheelchair user

Parapet   A parapet should be 60 cm high at most. To give a person in a wheelchair a good view, a window should not be divided by bars at eye level (approx. 125 cm). This often contradicts public regulations on the height of fall protection, meaning that constructive solutions, involving fencing the window off or reinforcing the glass, have to be found. > Fig. 37

Window arrangement   The accident risk can be reduced by arranging windows so that casements open towards walls or pieces of furniture rather than into transit areas. Windows divided into several openable casements are preferable to large single-casement windows. They should also be easy for a disabled person to clean.

Window types   <u>Turn/tilt windows</u> cannot always be opened by people with limited upper arm strength, and an opened casement may be dangerous to visually impaired people.

     <u>Horizontal sliding windows</u> are often a good option for disabled people, as they do not take up extra space when opened. They must, however, operate smoothly.

     <u>Skylights</u> should all be electrically operated or at least fitted with a rod linkage that can be operated by a wheelchair user and does not block movement areas.

     <u>Swing windows</u> (horizontally pivoted), or sash windows, which are pushed up to open, are not recommended.

Roller shutters and sun protection   Roller shutters (security shutters and light-excluding shutters) and other sun protection appliances must be operable. This usually involves an electrical system or mechanical linkage.

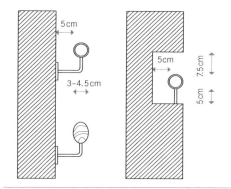

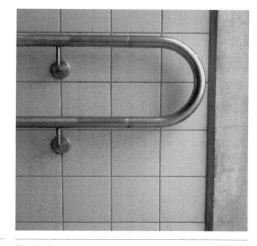

Fig. 38: Types of handrail and distance from the wall   Fig. 39: Double handrail for different users

Handrails, railings and wheel deflectors

Handrails, railings, grab handles and wheel deflectors can make it easier for disabled people to navigate walls, corridors and steps.

Handrails and railings are essential for stair and ramp areas. Hand- rails in hallways, or even in living and sanitary spaces, can also help disabled people. These aids should be mounted securely enough that a disabled person can lean their whole weight on them or use them to pull themselves up. In stair areas or long hallways, a handrail can also provide tactile guidance for blind or visually impaired people. Small raised symbols or changes in the thickness of the rail can notify users about which story they are on or about breaks in the route.

Handrails and railings

○

Users should be able to grasp the handrail safely and comfortably. Rails with a round or oval cross section of 30–45 mm at a sufficient distance from the wall are generally accepted. > Fig. 38

○ **Note:** When planning adequate movement areas, the clear area between two handrails must be taken into account as well as the spatial dimensions. Adding layers of plaster or handrails thus means the area is often well over the minimum dimensions prescribed for its unfinished state.

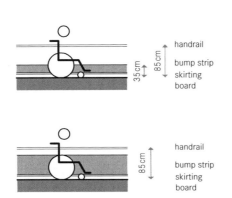

Fig. 40: Principles of horizontal bump strips   **Fig. 41: Wheel deflector as wall protection**

The ideal height for a handrail for wheelchair users is 85 cm, meaning that a second handrail, at the right height for walking adults, has to be installed to meet technical requirements for fall protection. > Figs. 38 and 39

Wheel deflectors and bump strips Where an edge or lip has to be made secure, wheel deflectors or guide plates are used. These should be 10–15 cm high. Different kinds of horizontal bump strips or wheel deflectors (e.g. a wooden board or a metal pipe) can also be applied to walls to prevent them from being damaged by chair wheels. > Figs. 40 and 41 Wall corner protection rails also protect areas where people move around.

IN-HOUSE SYSTEMS

Indoor climate Old people or those with impaired mobility are often more sensitive to the indoor climate than other people. They have a greater need for warmth due to their limited mobility, so the room must be warm enough for someone lying or sitting down. Blind or visually impaired people are in close contact with surfaces, making surface temperatures more important to them. A climate feels comfortable if the difference between air temperatures and surface temperatures is low. Older people in particular find cold surfaces—in a badly insulated house, for instance—as unpleasant as drafts.

A heating system that automatically adjusts the room temperature based on ambient temperature is a good idea, but users should be able to regulate any heating system independently and individually.

The user benefit of a home adapted for people with disabilities Electronic installation depends, among other things, on well-planned and functioning electrical systems. Electrical appliances and systems are particularly important in their day-to-day lives. All appliances in an electrical system suitable for disabled people should be, above all, independently operable and useable. Furthermore, these days many domestic utility items can be automated and digitally controlled using apps that are easy to operate.

Disabled people often have an increased need for security. An inter- Safety com system, with a video link, and lighting controlled by movement sensor provide peace of mind. A home emergency call service can be integrated into the telephone system. Emergency buttons in sanitary rooms may be advisable.

The movement space needed around all appliances, switches and Switches and sockets sockets has to be taken into account. Wheelchair users need controls to be at a height of 85 cm and at least 50 cm away from the wall of. > Fig. 20, page 26 Blind and visually impaired people, however, prefer controls to be installed at the usual height, where they are easier to find.

Buttons should be large and operate smoothly. Rocker switches should all work the same way (e.g. all turn downwards to switch the light off). Tactile marks on the buttons and a high-contrast design can also make them easier for visually impaired people to use.

Intercoms in apartments and doorbell systems in entrances should be easy for both children and wheelchair users to reach. The bell should also be located directly next to the door so that wheelchair users do not have to go far to reach it and to allow the door to be opened quickly. The tactile clarity of the doorbell panel is important for visually and hearing-impaired people. A door can be opened automatically without direct controls, so that the entrance door opens automatically when a resident approaches.

Lighting with no shadows or glare makes orientation easier for Room lighting visually impaired people. Lighting must be in place in the homes of blind people for any visitors, and it must be programmed to switch off automatically after a certain period of time.

Light sources with motion sensors are generally advisable for public buildings and access areas. This reduces construction costs, and also prevents people with impairments having to locate and get to light switches.

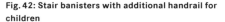

Fig. 42: Stair banisters with additional handrail for children

Fig. 43: Outdoor ramp with landing

Outdoor lighting   Good outdoor lighting is important to create a feeling of security and prevent accidents. It can be controlled by motion sensors or twilight switches.

ACCESS ELEMENTS

Vertical access   Vertical access within buildings is particularly important for wheelchair users, but also for blind or visually impaired people. In some circumstances, barrier-free stairs and ramps must be provided as well as lifts.

Stairs

Stairs   The length and width of steps should be based both on technical requirements and the anticipated users. A width of 135 cm allows more than one person to move up and down the stairs at the same time safely. A flight of stairs should not be too long, and should, if necessary, be interrupted by a landing. Seating on landings helps people who have difficulty in walking. The central stairwell gap should be as narrow as possible, and the flights of stairs should be close together, to prevent people from looking down and becoming dizzy. Where the space beneath the lowest landing of a staircase is less than 2.10 m high, a device must be fitted that prevents people from walking under such landings in order to prevent head injuries.

In places used by wheelchair users (e.g. in front of lifts), landings should be large enough that the movement areas for the stairs and for the lift do not overlap. A wheelchair user should always have an area of at least 150 cm × 150 cm in which to maneuver.

44

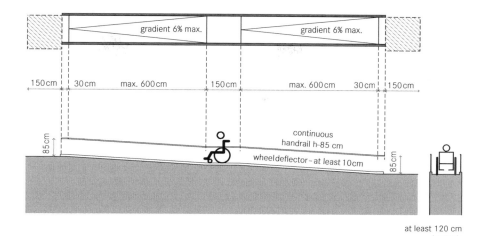

Fig. 44: Cross section and outline of a ramp suitable for wheelchair users

Emergency exit stairs must allow enough space for all wheelchair users resident in the building, so that the stairwell can provide areas for them to wait in safely until the fire brigade arrives.

A flight of stairs must be straight and have a regular gradient, allowing older and mobility-impaired people to use it comfortably and without stumbling. The treads should not project beyond the risers either, as this may cause users to catch their toes or heels on the upper step and stumble.

The surface design of the covering for the steps is also important. Floor covering > Chapter Construction and technical requirements, Construction components For visually impaired people in particular, it helps if the risers and treads are of different colors. Non-slip signal strips on the edge of the treads and special markings on the first and last steps of a flight also make a stair easier to use.

In addition to fall protection, continuous handrails must be fitted on Handrails both sides of the stair. To be easily graspable, the handrails should be at a height of 85 cm. > Chapter Construction and technical requirements, Construction components To guide blind people better, a handrail must extend 30 cm horizontally into the landing area. In buildings used by children, an additional, low handrail is a good idea. > Fig. 42

Ramps

Ramps are helpful to people with walking frames or pushchairs faced with a slight rise in ground level as well as wheelchair users. For wheelchair users, the gradient, along with the breadth of the ramp, is of pri-

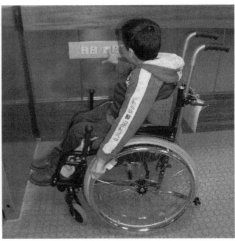

Fig. 45: Lift with call button suitable for wheelchair users

Fig. 46: Use of a lift by a wheelchair user

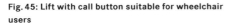

mary importance. The maximum practical gradient for an independently usable ramp is 6%. If the ramp is longer than 6 m, a horizontal landing of at least 150 cm should be provided, to give users the opportunity to rest. Ramps containing a sharp bend are difficult for wheelchair users to negotiate and should be avoided. Handrails at 85 cm are needed on both sides. These should project 30 cm beyond the ramp's beginning and end. Wheel deflectors at the sides with a height of at least 10 cm prevent wheelchairs from slipping off the ramp. > Chapter Construction components, Handrails, railings and wheel deflectors The wheel deflectors should not narrow the clearance width of the ramp—at least 120 cm. > Figs. 43 and 44

There should be no hazards such as traffic lanes, steps etc. in the extended area around a ramp. Ramps should also never be the only way of reaching an upper level—they should be accompanied by stairs or a lift, to offer a choice to users with limited mobility who are able to use stairs.

Lifts

Lifts enable wheelchair users, people with restricted mobility and older people to cope independently with multiple stories. They should be included in any public building or private apartment block. A lift must be constructed so that a disabled person can operate and use it independently. While private buildings need a lift only if they are four or five stories high, public buildings should ensure barrier-free access to all public rooms. It is also important for parking areas, especially underground garages, to be accessible by lift.

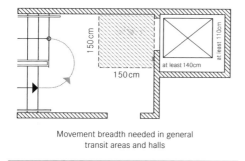

Movement breadth needed in general
transit areas and halls

Fig. 47: Area needed for wheelchairs in a stairwell in front of a lift

Dimensions

For wheelchairs, lifts need at least 1.10 m × 1.40 m clear space within their car. The lift shaft will be considerably larger, depending on the type of lift. A barrier-free lift must be reachable from public transit areas without a step up or down, and must stop on every level. It is advisable, and in many cases a legal requirement, to have at least one lift that can take wheeled stretcher carriers. This lift will need a clear space inside the car of at least 1.10 m × 2.10 m.

○

Lift doors

Lift doors should have a clear width of not less than 90 cm and should have light barriers, for safety purposes, across their whole height if possible. The gap between the shaft threshold and the car threshold must be as narrow as possible, to prevent walking sticks or Hoover canes from becoming trapped. The doors should also be power-operated and have a clear height of at least 210 cm. > Fig. 45

Movement areas

A movement area of at least 150 × 150 cm is needed in front of the lift, to allow queuing. If the lift door faces onto a stair exit, an area of 150 cm × 250 cm is needed to allow both wheelchair users and people on the stairs to use the facilities without difficulty. Wheelchair users who have driven forwards into smaller lifts will need enough space to turn if they have to exit the lift backwards. > Fig. 47

○ **Note:** For this reason, all escape staircases must be provided with spaces in addition to the required width of the escape route. These spaces can be used by wheelchair users to park there and wait for the rescue teams for help.

○ **Note:** Every country has its own specific regulations for the planning and operation of lifts. Technical and geometrical planning principles such as the width and height of the shaft, based on the dimensions of the car, can be obtained from the manufacturers.

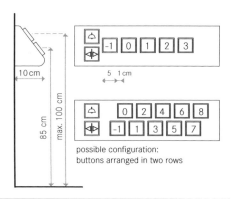

Fig. 48: Dimensions of a regulation horizontal control strip

Fig. 49: Horizontal control strip for wheelchair users

Controls should be easy for all users to reach, particularly wheelchair users and blind people. The control buttons must be about 50 mm in size with raised script or symbols (e.g. an alarm bell), so that they can be read by both blind and partially sighted people. The buttons should have a raised edge so that they can be read individually more easily and to prevent fingers from slipping.

Wheelchair users need an additional or alternative horizontal control panel that can be viewed from above. This should be at least 50 cm from the outer edge of the wheelchair and 85 cm above the floor. > Figs. 48 and 49 The control panel should be framed by a handrail to left and right, to give people with limited mobility a means of support. A mirror at the right height for a seated person set opposite the lift door helps wheelchair users to steer when exiting backwards.

For blind and visually impaired people in particular, there should be a second vertical control panel in the location where they would expect it to be. For the benefit of blind people, the optical signal announcing each story should be supplemented by an auditory signal.

Lifting platforms and stairlifts An integrated lifting platform designed specially for wheelchair users and people with limited mobility can help overcome minor differences in height (e.g. on an entrance landing). In listed buildings and private houses where lifts cannot be permanently installed, stairlifts with a seat that moves along the staircase are used.

Room plans

Other than barrier-free outdoor spaces and public buildings, > Chapter Outdoor facilities, Pavements and open spaces; Parking areas and garages an architect's planning assignments will largely involve the requirements for living spaces. The following chapters will therefore focus on private living space, although they could also be applied to homes for older people, restaurants etc. Exceptional situations in working environments and buildings open to the public will also be included.

BUILDING ENTRANCE AREAS

Barrier-free planning extends beyond the building to the area between the plot boundary and the building's entrance. In addition to paths, this may include parking spaces, play areas, gardens, refuse collection facilities and outdoor lighting.

○

The boxes in a mailbox unit must be within reach of wheelchair users, who should be able to drive right up to them. > Fig. 52   Mailboxes

In buildings used mainly by older people, an indoor mailbox unit could be decorated in different colors to make it easier to find the right box.

Shoescrapers should not be unattached to the ground, but should be inset and level with the floor covering. This reduces the risk of stumbling and allows wheelchair users to clean their wheels. The shoescraper should be long enough for the wheels to make a complete revolution.

In buildings where some residents have wheelchairs, wheelchair storage should be provided in the inner entrance area, between the outdoor space and living space. This should allow users to switch between two wheelchairs, especially if they use an electric wheelchair outdoors and a lighter and more maneuverable manually operated wheelchair indoors.   Storage space for wheelchairs or pushchairs

○ **Note:** Residents must be able to reach and fill refuse collection points outside the building themselves. Large refuse receptacles in particular must be set lower than the pavement. A wheelchair user can comfortably fill these to a height of 70 cm (Fig. 50).

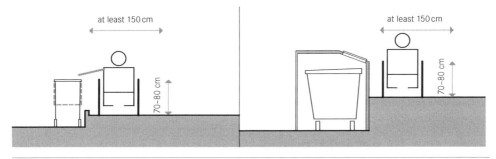

at least 150 cm

at least 150 cm

70–80 cm

70–80 cm

Fig. 50: Sunken refuse receptacle

Fig. 51: Reachability of mailbox units

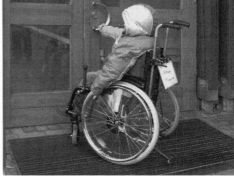

Fig. 52: Floor-level scraper in front of an entrance door

The storage space should therefore be large enough to allow transition from one wheelchair to the other. > Fig. 53 A socket with the control at 85 cm is needed for charging an electric wheelchair. Storage space for pushchairs should also be planned.

TRANSIT AREAS AND HALLS

Halls and other transit areas should always be free of obstacles. Open doors, window casements or projecting building parts in the transit space represent a barrier and are a hazard for visually impaired and blind people. A hall can be made largely obstacle-free by designing in niches around doors or specifying the direction in which doors and windows should open. In the halls of a residential building suitable for disabled people, wheelchair users should also be able to pass each other without difficulty, meaning that halls should be at least 150 cm and preferably 180 cm wide. > Fig. 54

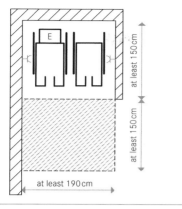

Fig. 53: Wheelchair storage and transition
area with maneuvering area

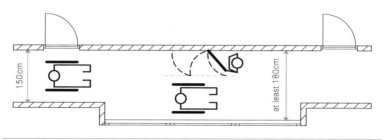

Fig. 54: Movement width needed in general transit areas and halls

Orientation can be improved by using a variety of materials for floor Orientation covering and giving walls contrasting designs. Lighting can also provide guidance, with different kinds of lighting identifying diverging routes, lifts and stairs.

ENTRANCE AREA OF HOMES

The entrance doors of private homes need adequate movement areas on both sides. > Chapter Construction and technical requirements, Construction components The inner entrance area behind the front door will include the hallway, the cloakroom and possibly a WC and storage room, as well as access to the other rooms. When planning for disabled people, areas must be laid out so that residents have plentiful freedom of movement even if the door is open—a wheelchair user needs a space of at least 160 cm × 160 cm to turn 360° if an open door is in the way. > Fig. 55

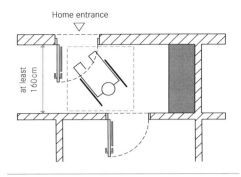

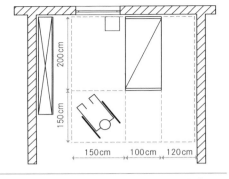

Fig. 55: Entrance area with cloakroom at the side

Fig. 56: Movement areas around bed of wheelchair user

The inner entrance area also includes the cloakroom and a shelf for keys and a telephone. If the entrance area is large it may require a handrail. A long narrow entrance area is inconvenient for a wheelchair user, as it is additionally obstructed by the cloakroom, for instance. Ideally there should be a side niche for the cloakroom and the shelf. > Fig. 55

LIVING AND SLEEPING SPACE

Living and leisure areas

Living areas for disabled people should above all be designed for independent living. Appliances can be a particular help to an individual achieving or enhancing their independence. Accidents must also be prevented. Cupboards and shelves at particular heights are often unusable by disabled people, especially wheelchair users. Swivel-mounted transverse compartments, carousels, adjustable floors and compartments, and extendable floors and clothes hanging rails can help to rectify this. Roll-up or sliding doors are easier to open. The furniture should be difficult to tip up and should tolerate being leant on.

Chairs and sofas should always be the same height as wheelchairs (46–48 cm) to allow easy transition. It should be possible for wheelchair users to get their legs underneath larger items of furniture while in the chair. Specifically, tables need to be approx. 80 cm high with a clear space of 67 cm underneath. Adjustable work surfaces are a good idea. All such items should also have a movement space of at least 150 cm between them and other furniture.

For blind people, a sense of homeliness is conveyed by senses other than sight, meaning that their living areas will be different from those of sighted people. Among other requirements, blind people need 80% more space for books due to the size of Braille script.

52

The bedroom is an especially peaceful and private place, and a place Bedrooms where disabled people often spend more time than non-disabled people, something that the room's design should reflect. In a care home, the bedroom may also be a private sitting room. Wheelchair users, blind and visually impaired people, and older people all need beds to be arranged in a different way. A wheelchair user needs a certain area of movement, depending on whether they get into bed at the side or lengthwise. > Fig. 56 Single beds for severely disabled people in need of care must be accessible from both sides. The movement area should be 150 cm deep on one side and 90 cm deep on the other side.

Patient lifts (or hoists), which can be directly connected with sanitary rooms, may have to be included in static ceiling load calculations. Additional light switches, alarm controls and sockets reachable from the bed should be included.

For practical and hygienic reasons, it may be a good idea or even essential to put the bedroom next to the sanitary space.

WORKING AREAS

Working area design should incorporate the access requirements and movement areas from the previous chapters. A personal working space in particular must be planned and designed for the abilities of a disabled employee.

With the exception of specialized workshops for disabled people, pro- Production site workspaces duction and workshop areas hardly ever contain barrier-free workspaces. These must be created where necessary. The work processes involved and, above all, the safety and accident prevention factors for a disabled person must be considered. People with impaired hearing, for instance, can only perceive dangers visually. Their workspaces should be positioned so that any possible sources of danger are in front of them, in their field of vision.

Office and computer workspaces in a home or work environment Office and computer workspaces must have an ergonomic design that enables the user to easily reach all tools and technological devices. As well as the need to fit wheelchairs under desks, it is important for wheelchair users and people with limited mobility to have all controls within reach.

Computer displays and inputs can be adapted to specific needs, but Communication communicating with non-disabled people can be a major problem in the world of work. Texts are not generally available in Braille or audiobook form, customers may not be used to interacting with disabled people, and deaf people may find telephone calls difficult. Braille keyboards, e-mail correspondence, computer programs that can convert text to speech or voice recognition software can help disabled and non-disabled people to

○ communicate.

BATHS AND SANITARY ROOMS

Sanitary rooms suitable for disabled people should be planned so that they can be used independently; as far as possible, without help. The arrangement of sanitary rooms within a home should, as far as possible, be adapted to the user's individual requirements. For instance, hallway access may make as much sense as bedroom access. If an additional WC for guests is planned, the priority should be arranging the main bath near the bedroom.

Sanitary facilities — Wheelchair users have particular requirements for movement areas, doors and thresholds, as well as sanitary objects and control mechanisms. > Chapter Construction and technical requirements

The right sanitary equipment, fittings and aids are crucial to disabled and older people. The dimensions for sanitary objects in public buildings can be adapted to individual needs in private homes. The planned room size should allow enough floor space for a washing machine and for bath fixtures. Underfloor heating makes the room more comfortable and does away with stumbling hazards such as rugs and mats.

Every sanitary object needs at least 150 × 150 cm movement space around it. As there will generally only be one person using a bath at a time, the movement areas can overlap. > Figs. 57 and 58

Showers — For people with limited mobility and wheelchair users in particular, there must be no step to prevent walking into or driving into the shower cubicle. The shower area is a movement area as well and should have a fold-out seat and several kinds of grab handle to enable transition out of and into the wheelchair. > Fig. 60 It is essential that the drain be level with the floor, with a slight gradient of 1–2% around it. A person should be able to reach the fittings while resting on the seat. The shower partitions should be arranged so as not to restrict free movement space. Easily moved shower curtains are the best way to prevent splashing.

○ **Note:** Barrier-free access to mass media and the Internet is particularly important for the independence of people with impairments. The World Wide Web Consortium has issued the Web Content Accessibility Guidelines to reduce Internet use barriers by, for instance, promoting easy-to-view websites with large print and symbols.

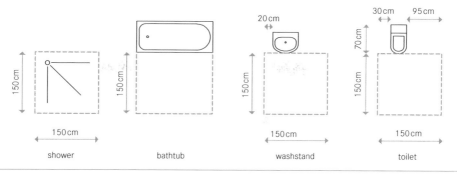

| shower | bathtub | washstand | toilet |

Fig. 57: Movement areas for shower, bathtub, WC and washbasin

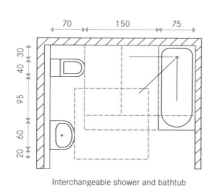

Interchangeable shower and bathtub

Fig. 58: Overlapping of movement areas in private bathing area with interchangeable shower and bathtub

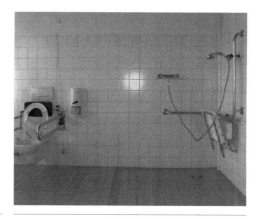

Fig. 59: Overlapping of movement space around shower and toilet

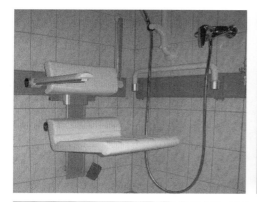

Fig. 60: Example of a shower seat suitable for a wheelchair user

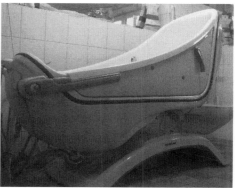

Fig. 61: Bathtub accessible to people with restricted mobility

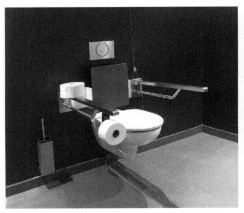

Fig. 62a: WC suitable for wheelchair users, accessible from both sides

Fig. 62b: Rest room suitable for wheelchair users; the washbasin is fitted high enough for the wheelchair user to get close.

Bathtubs   Bathtub use is difficult for wheelchair users and people with limited mobility. Getting in and out can however be made easier by mechanical aids such as lifts or hoists. Walk-in bathtubs or moveable bathtubs are also available. > Fig. 61 Grab handles are essential if a bathtub is to be used independently.

Washstands   For wheelchair users, washstands should have a height of approx. 80 cm. It must be possible to fit one's legs completely under them in a wheelchair, meaning that a clearance height of 67 cm within 30 cm of the
○   edge is needed. > Fig. 62

There should be grab or support bars on either side of a washbasin. These can also serve as towel rails. Placing a washstand low, at about 45-50 cm, makes fittings and soap dispensers easier to reach. All features such as storage space, soap dispensers etc. must be within reach. Mirrors should be set at the right height for someone in a wheelchair (lower edge at 90-100 cm). If it is to be used by several people, an adjustable washbasin may be a good idea.

> ○ Note: Special washstands for disabled people are available with flat siphons that avoid having plumbing underneath the washstand, which can get in the way. The need for higher inlets and outlets on the wall must be taken into account during planning.

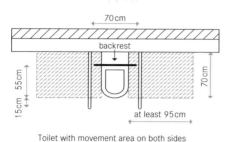

70 cm

backrest

55 cm

15 cm

70 cm

at least 95 cm

Toilet with movement area on both sides

Fig. 63: Public WC with grab and support bars and clearance space on both sides

The WC should have an elevated seat area of 46–48 cm to allow easy transition from and into wheelchairs and to make it easier for people with limited mobility to sit down and stand up. Arm supports that can be pushed up if necessary should also be fitted at a height of 85 cm on both sides. The distance between these handles should be 70 cm, and they should project 15 cm beyond the WC. The movement area around the WC should make it possible to get on or off from both sides (this may be necessary for people with one-sided paralysis). In private bathrooms it may be sufficient to provide movement space just on one side. > Fig. 63   O

Standard flushing apparatus such as flushing valves or cisterns are often hard for older or disabled people to activate. A button to operate the flush should therefore be mounted on the forward part of the support handle. If the sanitary facilities are primarily used by children or small people, low WCs and urinals at a height of about 48 cm should be planned for. In some facilities for small children, e.g. day nurseries, toilets are fitted at a height of between 26 and 40 cm for the purpose of training the children in the use of toilets.

O **Note:** Height-adjustable WCs can be set to any level up to 30 cm higher or lower. The height can be adjusted during use, which can also help the user to stand up. It is activated by remote control. Additionally, the overall depth of the WC should be 70 cm, to make transition easier.

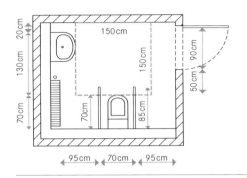
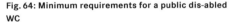

Fig. 64: Minimum requirements for a public dis-abled WC

Fig. 64a: Public rest room for the disabled

Controls Control fixtures such as bathroom fittings or toilet flushing controls should be fitted at a height of 85 cm, within easy reach. They should be easy to operate and have no sharp edges. Single faucets with an elongated handle or with motion sensors are easier to use independently. A temperature regulator can be incorporated to prevent scalding.

Public WC facilities WC facilities in public buildings and restaurants should have at least one unisex disabled toilet and a baby-changing facility with a low toilet for children. Requirements for WCs, washstands and mirrors are the same as those mentioned above, except that public toilet facilities should always have an emergency call system that can be reached from the toilet or from the floor. Furthermore, a floor drain should be in place to make cleaning easier. > Fig. 64

For WC facilities in parks, a greater surface area should be provided for users of electric wheelchairs. Radiators or pipe housing should not be allowed to encroach on the minimum surface area.

KITCHENS AND DINING ROOMS

Working processes Kitchen planning is all about the optimum organization of working processes. People with different disabilities need different kitchen plans, but many basic facts are the same. Every wide intervening space and vertical lifting process means that disabled or elderly people have to work harder, and makes orientation more difficult for blind people. Workspaces should therefore be concentrated together by organizing the kitchen elements in sequence. > Figs. 65 and 66

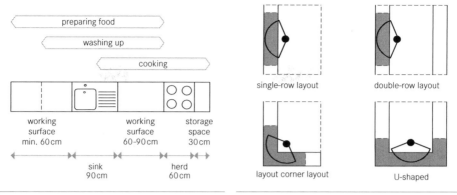

Fig. 65: Working processes and working spaces in the kitchen

single-row layout

double-row layout

layout corner layout

U-shaped

Fig. 66: Kitchen types and their respective working areas and movement radii

Due to the movement area needed, the kitchen space must not be too small. On the other hand, a large kitchen can make the work more difficult. Windows are also important in kitchen planning. In particular, windows above the worktop must be reachable by wheelchair user.

Kitchen space

Hazards such as sharp edges should be avoided, especially for blind and visually impaired people. When open, doors should have an angle of 180°, so as not to stick out into the room. Alternatively, they can be replaced by folding or sliding doors.

All control elements must be within easy reach of the user. >Chapter Types of barrier, Barriers to operating controls As electrical sockets are usually mounted on the wall above the worktop, wheelchair users often find them impossible to reach. An alternative would be to install these on the front of the worktop. A pull-out faucet is the usual choice for the washing-up area.

Items of furniture

Wheelchair users also need worktops and other furnishings they can get their legs beneath in a kitchen. > Fig. 67 Cookers installed at a low height allow wheelchair users to keep an eye on cooking pots. The height of worktops also depends on the locomotion and body size of the user. > Fig. 68 and Tab. 2

In this kind of planning for disabled people, there is often a lack of storage space due to the unavailability of high and low cupboards. So-called dispensary cupboards with pull-out drawers are roomy and save space. The cupboards should reflect the fact that it is particularly difficult for disabled people to reach anything lower than 30 cm from the ground.

Fig. 67: Sink unit for wheelchair users, with space beneath

Fig. 68: Low-set cooker for wheelchair user

Tab. 2: Working heights in relation to body size

Body size	Working height
Seated in wheelchair	70–80 cm (space underneath 67 cm)
155 cm	85 cm
160–165 cm	90 cm
170–175 cm	95 cm
180–185 cm	100 cm
190–200 cm	105 cm

Dining area   A dining area in the kitchen means that some kitchen work can be carried out on the dining table. A separate dining area should be accessible from the kitchen and from the living area. For hearing-impaired and deaf people in particular, a line of sight between the kitchen and living space also makes communication easier.

BALCONIES AND TERRACES

A ground-floor terrace or a balcony extends the living space of wheelchair users and people with limited mobility to include the outdoors, which might otherwise be very difficult to reach. Ground-level terraces provide easy access to outdoor path networks. Balconies or loggias, on the other hand, are more protective of the private sphere. Roofing over

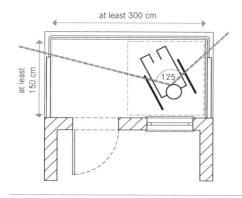

Fig. 69: Minimum surface area of a balcony for wheelchair users

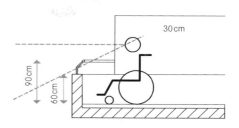

Fig. 70: Balcony with two-part parapet for wheelchair users

and weather protection on each side prevent people from looking in and allow access to the open air even in variable weather. If the feature faces south or west, it should have adequate sun protection.

Movement areas have to be taken into account for outdoor areas, with wheelchair users needing more space than other users. It is also advisable to provide enough space for chairs and a table and give the user as wide a view of the surroundings as possible. > Fig. 69

Size

The parapet must satisfy fall protection requirements and provide the occupant with a sense of security. At the same time, wheelchair users should have as clear a view as possible. > Fig. 70

Parapet height

Doors to balconies and terraces should have easily operated handles. The 15 cm step generally needed for insulation can often be achieved without blocking independent access to the outdoor area by using construction details (such as covered gutters that can be easily driven over). > Chapter Construction and technical requirements, Construction components

Outdoor facilities

As people of all ages and levels of ability use streets and outdoor areas, they must satisfy universal requirements.

In practice, this is often made difficult by the topographic situation, the unplanned nature of historic streets, and other constraints. However, it is always a good idea to consider how conditions in any location can be upgraded to minimize barriers or provide ways round them.

PAVEMENTS AND OPEN SPACES

Planning factors affecting pavement accessibility are:

— pavement width
— longitudinal and lateral gradients
— covering material
— curb placement and formation
— the arrangement of orientation aids > Chapter Outdoor guidance systems

Large open spaces are a special case, as these can make orientation difficult for visually impaired people. Green areas and play areas should also be designed so that everyone can use them independently.

Minimum width for pavements

Pavements should be at least 150 cm wide. A wider pavement (at least 165 cm) makes it easier to control a wheelchair on non-level ground, and a width of 180–200 cm allows two wheelchairs to pass each other. > Fig. 71

Gradient

For wheelchair users, the longitudinal gradient should not be greater than 6%. In this respect, the need for a barrier-free pavement may conflict with the need for gutters to prevent accumulation of rainwater. Gutters must be shallow enough to be easily driven over. Alternatively, a slight transverse gradient, not severe enough to cause steering problems for wheelchair users, could be planned in. Paths with a lateral slope must include fall protection.

Curbs

The curb is a major obstacle to people with restricted mobility, and especially to wheelchair users. To allow it to be easily driven over, it must be lowered by 2 cm, but it should remain detectable to a blind person's cane. A curb design that differs from the ground covering is also helpful to visually impaired people. Footpaths and cycle paths must also be easy to tell apart. In green areas, markers at the sides of paths, e.g. stones

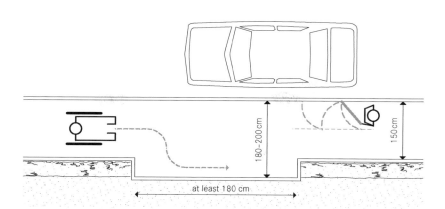

at least 180 cm

180-200 cm

150 cm

Fig. 71: Meeting places on pavements

around the edges of lawns, enable blind people to feel their way along paths.

Barriers and barricades are difficult for blind people to detect using canes, as they often do not reach the ground and the cane therefore passes under them. An additional horizontal barrier at or near floor level, or warning markings set into the ground beneath the barrier, reduce this risk. Barriers and barricades

Bollards and similar fixtures must be 100 cm apart to allow wheelchairs to pass through. They should also be tall enough to be detected by a blind or visually impaired person's cane, to reduce the risk of tripping over them. For the same reason, there must be no obstacles at head height, as these cannot be detected by cane and may cause severe injuries. Badly secured roadworks are a major source of danger if blind people are not aware of their presence on a familiar route. > Chapter Planning requirements, Planning for visually impaired and blind people

Older people and people with limited mobility in particular appreciate regular rest areas and seating. In inner-city and park areas, there should ideally be a bench every 100 m. A stowage space for wheelchairs, pushchairs etc. should be provided next to the bench. > Fig. 76 Seating in rest areas

Paths with a lateral gradient must have fall protection. If the incline is between 4% and 6%, level rest spaces for wheelchair users should be provided every 6–10 m.

Fig. 72: Combined non-step curb edge and warning strip

Fig. 73: Curb edge impassable to wheelchair users

Fig. 74: Cordon marking the end of a path: not detectable by the Hoover cane

Fig. 75: Secured construction trench at a road intersection: a hazard for blind people

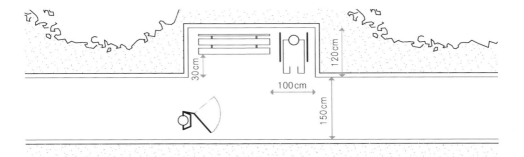

Fig. 76: Outdoor bench niche with space for wheelchair

Fig. 77: Grooves in front of platform edge   **Fig. 78: Alert strip at a bus stop**

Only non-slip, high-grip and flat-laying materials should be used as   Coverings
coverings. They must provide enough grip to shoes and wheelchairs even
if the surface is dirty, wet or covered by snow. Concrete slabs, poured
asphalt or similar coverings are standard. The structure should not be
too coarse, however, as this increases friction on chair wheels.

Varying the materials or laying patterns in the paving helps orientation.

OUTDOOR GUIDANCE SYSTEMS
Guidance systems and floor indicators help visually impaired people
to find their way around outdoor areas, particularly where there is an
increased need for safety, such as on railway platforms. > Figs. 77 and 78

Guidance lines, delineating strips, marker strips and hazard warning
surfaces are used to flag up and identify changes of direction and haz-
ardous areas.

Guidance lines or delineating strips designate a path. These are strips   Guidance lines
of ground surface indicator tiles with grooves, 25–60 cm wide. The
grooves should always run in the direction of travel. They are easiest to
detect when laid in smoothly paved areas. The start and finish of the guidance system must be marked with an alert strip approximately 90 x 90 cm
wide or a marker strip across the whole width of the path. >Figs. 81 and 82

Guidance lines also help people to keep their distance from traffic lanes and railways. They should be 50–60 cm from the edge. If the guidance lines are being laid in a narrow place, they may be laid 30 cm from the edge. They must be 50 cm away from any fixed objects.

Hazard warning surfaces Hazard warning surfaces flag up diverging routes, changes of direction, changes in ground level or information boards. They should be noticeably broader than guidance lines (at least 60 cm wide, and preferably 90 cm wide). > Fig. 82 Blister paving makes a particularly good hazard warning surface, as it has a non-directional surface. Hazard warning surface material should be easily detectable to the feet. Different material (an elastic material, for instance) or a conspicuous surface structure (such as blister slabs) are used to distinguish hazard warning surfaces from guidance lines. Blisters of 4–5 mm in height are easy for the foot or cane to detect. > Fig. 81 In addition to these hazard warnings, marker strips across the pavement make crossings easier to find (marking traffic light controls, for instance).

Guidance system materials Guidance systems can be constructed using concrete slabs, ceramic tiles and slabs, hard rubber, metal or natural stone. The acoustic and visual properties as well as the tactile properties must be different from the surrounding covering.

To aid visual detection, the luminosity of ground surface indicators must contrast with that of the surrounding paving.

○ **Note:** In a street with no guidance system, blind people use other tactile elements and edges to orient themselves. However, these are often blocked by street furniture, billboards, parked bicycles etc., creating potential hazards (Figs. 79 and 80).

Fig. 79: Obstacles blocking a path marked by tactile paving

Fig. 80: Boards and obstacles along the edge of the paving

Fig. 81: Guidance line and hazard warning surfaces with different surface structures

Fig. 82: Hazard warning surface in front of a turn-off

Auditory signals, as well as floor-level guidance systems, are needed in the street—to tell visually impaired people which phase the traffic lights are at, for instance. Traffic lights are fitted with <u>clocks</u> and <u>vibration</u> plates that can be detected by blind or visually impaired people. The clocks emit a regular signal sound that helps to locate the traffic lights. This changes perceptibly when the light is at green. > Figs. 83 and 84 Vibrating plates provide additional support for people with impaired vision or hearing. The outer plate vibrates when the lights are at green.

Fig. 83: Beeper on a traffic light

Fig. 84: Traffic light system with tactile and acoustic guidance

Signal devices must be aligned along the crossing's middle axis. At pedestrian and cyclist crossing with the same signaling devices, these should be located at the boundaries of both crossings.

The direction of travel is marked by a raised, tactile arrow on the lower edge of the signaling device, where alerts on rail traffic, other activating buttons and traffic island alerts can also be provided.

The movement area on a traffic island should be at least 300–400 cm wide and 250 cm deep, to allow wheelchair users to cross safely.

PARKING AREAS AND GARAGES

Placement of disabled parking spaces

Disabled parking spaces should be provided for private homes and for public buildings—where 3–5% of spaces should be reserved for disabled drivers. At any rate, public buildings should have at least one disabled parking space, which must be clearly marked by a wheelchair symbol. > Fig. 85

> ○ **Note:** Controlled pedestrian crossing describes a pedestrian facility with a traffic light or other crossing aid, as opposed to a non-controlled pedestrian crossing with a zebra strip.

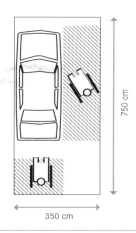

750 cm

350 cm

Fig. 85: Designated disabled parking space with a ramp for pavement access

Fig. 86: Parking space suitable for disabled people, with movement areas

It is not only disabled people who have specific parking needs. Parents accompanied by children also appreciate a larger parking bay— dealing with children and pushchairs requires a larger space alongside the vehicle, just as wheelchairs do.

Disabled parking spaces should be as close as possible to the building's entrance or the parking facility's exit, both of which should be easily accessible, with curbs at a height of 3 cm and optically marked to help users cover the distance independently in a wheelchair.

A disabled parking space must be extra large. As well as accommodating the vehicle, it must allow users to transfer into a wheelchair. It should therefore be at least 350 cm wide, and should also be longer to allow the car's boot to be unloaded from the wheelchair. The parking area should therefore be at least 750 cm in length. > Fig. 86

Arrangement – dimensions

Where several disabled parking spaces are arranged vertically, the space in between can be used by two wheelchair users. > Fig. 87 Disabled parking spaces arranged parallel to a road lane, on the other hand, only make sense if the driver is able to get out on the side that faces the road. Otherwise, the car must be far enough away from the road for the driver to alight without danger. The gradient must also be level to prevent any rolling toward the road. As with other disabled spaces, the space must be long enough for the car's boot to be reached from a wheelchair. > Fig. 88

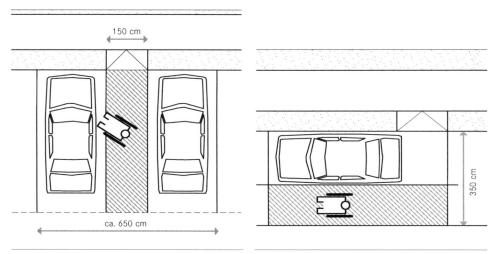

Fig. 87: Vertical arrangement with shared space for getting out

Fig. 88: Parking space arranged parallel to traffic

Garages

Single-user garage plans must allow enough space. Garage doors for private garages should always be automatic, with a remote control.

Multi-story or underground garages need a lift suitable for disabled people. The disabled parking spaces should be on the ground floor of a multi-story facility, enabling evacuation of wheelchair users and mobility-impaired people in case of fire, when lifts would be out of action. As control elements such as ticket machines are often impossible for disabled people in a car to reach, disabled parking spaces in multi-story car parks or underground garages can also be placed in front of the barrier.

Orientation

In large garages in particular, a parking guidance system to aid orientation is a good idea. This should show where easy-access parking spaces are located, as well as indicating empty parking spaces. Floor and wall markings, color schemes or specifically positioned lighting elements can improve orientation. Floor markings can also be used to guide pedestrians to lifts, stairwells and exits.

In conclusion

There is more to barrier-free planning and construction than regulations and statements of requirements. It expresses a basic belief in social integration for everyone. Beyond the technical methods described here, <u>Design for All</u> really means answering the day-to-day needs and requirements of people with impairments, with the focus on recognizing and eliminating barriers. Promoting sensitivity to the needs of disabled people is a far-reaching social issue.

Architects and engineers, whose plans have a major role in shaping people's everyday surroundings, can create the right conditions for a world with minimal barriers. General planning advice and parameters applying to the specific situation contained in regulations and in law must be consulted. There are, however, no cut-and-dried barrier-free planning solutions. The planner should try to find individual, long-term solutions tailored to the user and the construction project. While barrier-free buildings help the target group, their flexibility and sustainability also benefit all users.

Appendix

LITERATURE

Christian Schittich (ed.): *In Detail: Housing for People of All Ages,* Birkhäuser, Basel 2007

Oliver Herwig: *Universal Design: Solutions for Barrier-free Living,* Birkhäuser, Basel 2008

James Homes-Siedle: *Barrier-Free Design: A Manual for Building Designers and Managers,* Architectural Press, New York 1996

Wendy A. Jordan: *Universal Design Home: Great-Looking, Great-Living Design for All Ages, for the Abilities, and Circumstances,* Rockport Publishers, Beverly/MA 2008

REGULATIONS AND STANDARDS

International Standards

E ISO 3864	Graphical symbols—Safety colours and safety signs
ISO 4190-5	Lift (elevator) installation—Control devices, signals and additional fittings
ISO 21542	Building construction—Accessibility and usability of the built environment
EN ISO 9999	Assistive products for persons with disability—Classification and terminology
EN ISO 10535	Hoists for transfer of disabled persons
ISO/TR 11548-1	Communication aids for blind persons—Identifiers, names and assignation to coded character sets for 8-dot Braille characters—Part 1: General guidelines for Braille identifiers and shift marks
ISO/TS 16071	Ergonomics of human-system interaction—guidance on accessibility for human-Computer interfaces
28 CFR Part 36 (USA)	Nondiscrimination on the Basis of Disability by Public Accommodations and in Commercial Facilities; ADA Standards for Accessible Design
EN 81-70	Safety rules for the construction and installations of lifts
EN 614-1	Safety of machinery—Ergonomic design principles—Terminology and general principles
EN 12182	Technical aids for disabled person
EN 12217	Doors—Operating forces—Requirements and classification
EN 12464	Light and lighting—Lighting of work places
prEN 15209	Specification for Tactile Paving Surface Indicators
EN 60849	Sound systems for emergency purposes (IEC 100/540/CDV)
DIN EN 17210	Accessibility and usability of the built environment—Functional requirements; prEN 17210:2019
EU Directive 2016/2102	on the accessibility of the websites and mobile applications of public sector bodies

PICTURE CREDITS
Cover: David Hollnack
Figs. 7, 27, 34, 35, 46, 59, 68: Birgit Wehner, Felsenmeerschule,
    LWL-Förderschule in Hemer
Fig. 8: Adrian Simut, London
Figs. 10, 12, 30, 41, 49, 51, 62, 73, 84: Lea Böhme, Michael U. Grotz
Figs. 14,15, 26, 42: Rahel Züger, AWO Kita Schalthaus Beisen, Essen,
    Germany
Figs. 16, 17: Bestrossi, www.wikimedia.de
Fig. 77: www.wikimedia.de
Figs. 60, 61, 67: Hayo Harms, Zentrum für Körperbehinderte,
    Wohnanlage Kilianshof, Würzburg; Germany

All other figures by the authors. Special thanks go to Adrian Simut
for his assistance with drawings.

THE AUTHORS
    Isabella Skiba, Dipl.-Ing., freelance architect in Dortmund, Germany
    Rahel Züger, Dipl.-Ing., architect in Dortmund and Essen, Germany

ALSO AVAILABLE FROM BIRKHÄUSER:

Design

Basics Design and Living
Jan Krebs
ISBN 978-3-7643-7647-5

Basics Office Design
Bert Bielefeld
ISBN 978-3-0356-1394-0

Basics Design Ideas
Bert Bielefeld, Sebastian El khouli
ISBN 978-3-7643-8112-7

Basics Design Methods
Kari Jormakka
ISBN 978-3-03821-520-2

Basics Materials
M. Hegger, H. Drexler, M. Zeumer
ISBN 978-3-7643-7685-7

Basics Spatial Design
Ulrich Exner, Dietrich Pressel
ISBN 978-3-7643-8848-5

Available as a compendium:
Basics Architectural Design
Bert Bielefeld (ed.)
ISBN 978-3-03821-560-8

Fundamentals of Presentation

Basics Architectural Photography
Michael Heinrich
ISBN 978-3-7643-8666-5

Basics CAD
Jan Krebs
ISBN 978-3-7643-8109-7

Basics Freehand Drawing
Florian Afflerbach
ISBN 978-3-03821-545-5

Basics Detail Drawing
Bert Bielefeld (ed.)
ISBN 978-3-0356-1392-6

Basics Freehand Drawing
Florian Afflerbach
ISBN 978-3-03821-545-5

Basics Modelbuilding
Alexander Schilling
ISBN 978-3-0356-2182-2

Basics Technical Drawing
Bert Bielefeld, Isabella Skiba
ISBN 978-3-0346-1326-2

Available as a compendium:
Basics Architectural Presentation
Bert Bielefeld (ed.)
ISBN 978-3-03821-527-1

Construction

Basics Concrete Construction
Katrin Hanses
ISBN 978-3-0356-0362-0

Basics Facade Apertures
Roland Krippner, Florian Musso
ISBN 978-3-7643-8466-1

Basics Glass Construction
Andreas Achilles, Diane Navratil
ISBN 978-3-7643-8851-5

Basics Loadbearing Systems
Alfred Meistermann
ISBN 978-3-7643-8107-3

Basics Masonry Construction
Nils Kummer
ISBN 978-3-7643-7645-1

Basics Roof Construction
Ann-Christin Siegemund
978-3-0356-1942-3

Basics Steel Construction
Katrin Hanses
ISBN 978-3-0356-0370-5

Basics Timber Construction
Ludwig Steiger
ISBN 978-3-0356-2126-6

Available as a compendium:
Basics Building
Construction
Bert Bielefeld (ed.)
ISBN 978-3-0356-0372-9

**Building Services/
Building Physics**
Basics Fire Safety
Diana Helmerking
ISBN 978-3-0356-1859-4

Basics Lighting Design
Roman Skowranek
ISBN 978-3-0356-0929-5

Basics Electro-Planning
Peter Wotschke
ISBN 978-3-0356-0932-5

Basics Room Conditioning
Oliver Klein, Jörg Schlenger
ISBN 978-3-7643-8664-1

Basics Water Cycles
Doris Haas-Arndt
ISBN 978-3-7643-8854-6

Available as a compendium:
Basics Building Technology

Bert Bielefeld (ed.)
ISBN 978-3-0356-0928-8

Professional Practice
Basics Project Control
Pecco Becker
ISBN 978-3-0356-1666-8

Basics Budgeting
Bert Bielefeld, Roland Schneider
ISBN 978-3-03821-532-5

Basics Construction Scheduling
Bert Bielefeld
ISBN 978-3-7643-8873-7

Basics Site Management
Lars-Phillip Rusch
ISBN 978-3-0356-1607-1

Basics Tendering
Tim Brandt,
Sebastian Th. Franssen
ISBN 978-3-7643-8110-3

Basics Time Management
Bert Bielefeld
ISBN 978-3-7643-8873-7

Available as a compendium:
Basics Project Management
Architecture
Bert Bielefeld (ed.)
ISBN 978-3-03821-462-5

Urbanism
Basics Urban Analysis
Gerrit Schwalbach
ISBN 978-3-7643-8938-3

Basics Urban Building Blocks
Thorsten Bürklin, Michael Peterek
ISBN 978-3-7643-8460-9

Available at your bookshop or at www.birkhauser.com

Series editor: Bert Bielefeld
Concept: Bert Bielefeld, Annette Gref
Translation from German into English:
Michael Robinson
English copy editing: Monica Buckland
Project management: Annette Gref
Layout, cover design and typography:
Andreas Hidber
Typesetting and production: Amelie Solbrig

Paper: Magno Natural, 120 g/m²
Print: Beltz Grafische Betriebe GmbH

Library of Congress Control Number:
2020938912

Bibliographic information published by the
German National Library
The German National Library lists this publica-
tion in the Deutsche Nationalbibliografie;
detailed bibliographic data are available on the
Internet at http://dnb.dnb.de.

ISBN 978-3-0356-2192-1
e-ISBN (PDF) 978-3-0356-2193-8
e-ISBN (EPUB) 978-3-0356-2194-5
German Print-ISBN 978-3-0356-2183-9

© 2020 Birkhäuser Verlag GmbH, Basel
P.O. Box 44, 4009 Basel, Switzerland
Part of Walter de Gruyter GmbH, Berlin/Boston

9 8 7 6 5 4 3 2 1

www.birkhauser.com